the
DESIGN
MUSEUM

50

MEN'S
FASHION
ICONS
**THAT CHANGED
THE WORLD**

DAN
JONES

conran
OCTOPUS

MEN'S
FASHION
ICONS

INTRODUCTION

Meet the stylish men of music, art, film and literature, power-dressing politicians and counterculture revolutionaries. These are the influencers whose unique ways of dressing have inspired whole genres of contemporary fashion; 50 male style icons who embody that near-indefinable thing: a sense of cool.

Some maintain a confident simplicity – finding a look and sticking with it – creating a timeless way of dressing as relevant today as it was in decades past. That enduring preppy, heritage style? Look to JFK's off-duty deck-out. Skinny jeans, T-shirt and scuffed Converse? Here's to Johnny Ramone. Others take a sharp left turn from the mainstream, from the pomp and fizz of Stephen Tennant, the original Bright Young Thing, and Grayson Perry's alter ego Claire, to the late, great David Bowie in the vibrant stage outfits of designer Kansai Yamamoto.

Across the decades there are shared themes and reoccurring garments – perfectly cut suiting, wonderfully worn-in jeans, Breton stripes, the classic T-shirt – and more than a few surprises. Tom Wolfe's trademark white suit and John Waters's pop-colour dressing break sartorial codes in subtle ways, and maverick architect Peter Marino's slick leather fetish wear thrillingly rejects them completely. For every man in this book who toes the line, there is another who moonwalks over it.

Marlon Brando as leather-clad biker Johnny Strabler in a publicity portrait for *The Wild One* (Laslo Benedek, 1953). As Strabler, Brando's style – denim, biker jacket, white T-shirt – became the unofficial uniform of an alienated, angry youth.

STEPHEN TENNANT

The brightest of the Bright Young Things, British aristocrat Stephen Tennant (1906–87) was a true English eccentric. Born into nobility, Tennant cut a dazzling figure in the gossipy bohemian society satirized by Evelyn Waugh in *Vile Bodies* (1930). In the late 1920s and early 1930s tabloids obsessively reported on Tennant and his gang's glittering pre-war debauchery powered by champagne, madcap treasure hunts and what P G Wodehouse described as 'naughty salt'.

Tennant's class and wealth made him seemingly untouchable by critique, and his unique sense of style – unbound by gender – was wonderfully indulgent. Iconic portraits by a young Cecil Beaton show Tennant as a suited, spindle-thin young man with delicate finger waves set into fine hair, a dusting of make-up, lipstick and a glossy overcoat, collar up – just a hint of the sartorial flamboyance for which he was known.

Inspiring any number of literary characters – not least, Sebastian in Waugh's *Brideshead Revisited* (1945) – Tennant romanced Siegfried Sassoon, commanded audiences with Jean Genet and Greta Garbo, and nursed a love of leopard-print pyjamas and chinchilla collars. When he notoriously took to his bed during the final 17 years of his life, he allowed the great and the good, including Christopher Isherwood and David Hockney, to continue to visit. By the 1980s Tennant's eccentricity knew few bounds. The last photographs of the aristocrat show him in bed like royalty, hair dyed cerise, surrounded by jewels, sketches and postcards.

Cecil Beaton's dramatic 1927 portrait captures Tennant's theatrical, otherworldly spirit (the young aesthete adored a costume party) as well as his somewhat frail-looking countenance: melodramatic, mournful eyes, hair in soft waves, dark lipstick and make-up from the powder puff he kept in his gold cigarette case.

Tennant defied traditional gender expectations, less as a political statement and more as an instinctive expression. Not many could wear a pleated wool skirt styled with a wide-brimmed hat, but Tennant's unshakeable social standing meant he could get away with it.

FRED ASTAIRE

The charming and athletic top-hat-and-tails-wearing dancer, actor and *bon vivant* Fred Astaire (1899–1987) was born in Nebraska and was a performer from the age of six. Considered one of the world's finest showmen, notably for his tap dancing, Astaire starred in classic Hollywood musicals for four decades, from *Top Hat* (1935) to *Finian's Rainbow* (1968).

After a move to New York in 1905, Astaire – along with his sister Adele – sang and danced in a vaudeville double act, eventually working on Broadway and in London's West End until the act ended with Adele's marriage in 1932. Astaire's physical appearance made his move into film difficult – he was arguably not conventionally handsome enough to be a leading man – but his dancing skills overcame that. He was partnered with Ginger Rogers, first in *Flying Down to Rio* (1933), and the pair made nine films in all, each an important moment in musical cinema.

Perfect dressing, to Astaire, meant taking his suit back to the tailor at least six times, as he told *Gentlemen's Quarterly* in 1957, and its design and fabric, he thought, should be conservative – inconspicuous, even. This fastidious approach meant his personal style was formal and well honed, but he allowed himself the occasional flash in a pair of jewelled cufflinks and an unfolded pocket square. His footwear collection included more than 50 professional dancing shoes.

Fred Astaire's slow yet steady rise to celebrity was marked by his refined, suited look – he became Hollywood's all-singing, all-dancing, top-hat-and-tails-wearing performer. As a one-time child star, Astaire grew up in the limelight – no wonder he looked so at home in it.

FRED PERRY

Frederick John Perry (1909–95) was the first British sports celebrity, a tennis champion who transformed the game, winning Wimbledon on three consecutive years from 1934, and the first player to win all four Grand Slam titles – the Wimbledon, Australian, French and American championships. He was also the founder of one of the world's most successful sports-inspired lifestyle brands. Throughout his professional career Perry balanced the opposing forces of sport and commerce, but was often at odds with traditional sports institutions that frowned upon his commercial success even as he grew as a world-class athlete.

In 1936 Perry left the UK to tour the United States, earning some impressive fees, but soon found himself banned from prestigious Lawn Tennis Association events in his home country because of this. After World War II, Perry's entrepreneurial spirit led him to transform the traditional, staid sportswear of tennis players. During his Wimbledon wins Perry had used medical gauze around his wrist to absorb sweat, and, with Austrian footballer Tibby Wegner, he put a towelling version into production in the late 1940s. The success of the sweatband saw Perry and Wegner move on to create slim-fitting tennis shirts, and the iconic Fred Perry polo shirt went into production in 1952.

Perry transformed not only the game of tennis itself, but also the style of the players on court. His designs – slimmed-down versions of the impractical, baggy tennis whites of old – had an easy functionality, designed by an experienced player. There was a sense of excitement around the brand, as Perry's succession of wins and fame in the United States saw him move in celebrity circles. There is a photograph of Perry taken in 1934, sunning himself, bare-chested and smiling, with Marlene Dietrich by his side.

As his fame grew in America and relations with the UK tennis establishment became strained, tennis champion Fred Perry found himself up against fellow Briton Jack Crawford at the 1933 US National Championship Tournament in New York. Dressed in the traditional baggy tennis whites that he would later transform with his sportswear brand, Perry fought hard for the title and won.

Impeccably groomed screen legend William Clark Gable (1901–60) famously delivered the caustic final line of Hollywood classic *Gone with the Wind* (1939). Before walking off into the mist in a pristine charcoal-grey suit, his face framed by a sharp white shirt collar, he utters the words, 'Frankly, my dear, I don't give a damn.' As the unofficial 'king of Hollywood', Gable is the actor at the heart of some of the most iconic moments in cinematic history.

As a young man, Gable took acting classes, fixed his teeth and hair, and worked to lower the pitch of his voice. Then came work as an extra, bit parts in silent films and theatre plays, and, finally, a contract with MGM, for which he played unshaven on-screen villains. The studio helped to establish his popularity, pairing him with well-known female stars, smoothing out his appearance and garnering Gable a reputation as something of a lothario. He became a leading man in more than 60 classic films, from *Mutiny on the Bounty* (1935) to his final work, *The Misfits* (1961), with Marilyn Monroe.

The actor's publicity photographs show a plethora of suiting in high-grade wools and tweeds, high-waisted slacks with pleats and classic blazers with wide lapels and workwear patch pockets. His casual looks were smart by contemporary standards – a shirt and tie with a V-neck sweater – and Gable's groomed appearance included perfectly slicked-back hair and a small manicured moustache. He was rarely without a pocket square or a fresh carnation or rose in his buttonhole.

Cutting a perfect sartorial silhouette, Clark Gable's official 1930s portraits show the actor in various power poses. The sharp angles of double-breasted suits in dark, rich fabrics with exaggerated lapels and shoulder pads were a key part of the meticulously constructed, moody imagery that was used to glamorize and market the actor, then at the height of his fame.

HUMPHREY BOGART

As Hollywood's laid-back star of film noir, Humphrey Bogart (1899–1957) played the hard-boiled detective embedded in dark mysteries and murderous plots, dealing with a missing jewel-encrusted artifact (*The Maltese Falcon*, 1941) or a series of dangerous *femmes fatales* (*The Big Sleep*, 1946, and *Dark Passage*, 1947). For his efforts, Bogart is thought of as the greatest male star of classic Hollywood cinema.

A New York City native, Bogart spent time in the navy before becoming a stalwart on Broadway: a jobbing stage actor of questionable talent. Gaining experience, he was cast in the hit film *The Petrified Forest* (1936), followed by *High Sierra* (1941) and then *The Big Sleep* (1946) and *Key Largo* (1948).

Bogart's style – on and off screen – was defined by suited, uncomplicated looks that suggested a quiet authority. Chunky double-breasted pinstripe suits were his private-detective garb; the white tuxedo jacket and the fedora and belted trench coat the actor wore in *Casablanca* (1942) are particularly iconic. But it was his mastery of understated style that resounds, reflected somewhat in his strong, pared-down performances.

Bogart married actress and co-star Lauren Bacall in 1945; Bacall was a style icon in her own right, and the pair was considered Hollywood royalty. Each official photograph of Bogart was carefully posed to give the rather short actor a more impressive stature. In 1955 Bogart and Bacall, along with Frank Sinatra, Angie Dickinson, Judy Garland and others, founded the original incarnation of the Rat Pack, an informal group of celebrity hell-raisers who became notorious in the press.

Warner Bros Studios' official portraits of Humphrey Bogart were careful to underline the laid-back, brooding nature synonymous with his on-screen roles – to the public, he was one and the same as his tough, film noir characters. This shot from 1939 shows Bogart in classic wool tweed textured suiting, worn with an unbuttoned shirt and unfolded pocket square; a relaxed look that has a quiet authority.

ALBERT CAMUS

Football-loving winner of the 1957 Nobel Prize for Literature, the French writer Albert Camus (1913–1960) was the master of insouciant style: trench coat with upturned collar, slicked-back hair and a never-ending cigarette. Camus worked with political resistance organizations, and his impressive catalogue of writings, from essays to novels and plays, includes novels *The Stranger* (1942) and *The Plague* (1947).

Camus's childhood in Algeria did little to instil a sense of hope; he was born in poverty and surrounded by melancholy. Attending university, Camus wrote of his experiences as goalkeeper for the junior team of Le Racing universitaire d'Alger, enjoying the camaraderie and unabashed team spirit of the game, but tuberculosis cut his sporting career short. His published writings are greatly influenced by Algeria and its experience of French colonialism, and with each new work Camus marked himself out as an outspoken and passionate philosophical and political thinker.

That cliché of nostalgic Parisian style – smoking outside the Café de Flore or Les Deux Magots on the Left Bank, looking effortlessly cool – can be linked to Camus and his contemporaries Jean-Paul Sartre and Simone de Beauvoir, all of whom did just that in the 1940s and 1950s. Camus was a simple, confident dresser: he wore thick wool jackets and slacks, dishevelled shirts and loosely knotted ties; his iconic trench coat completed his writer's uniform.

This portrait of the great philosopher, writer and former footballer from 1945 shows him at legendary literary haunt Les Deux Magots in Saint-Germain-des-Prés, Paris. Although Camus was one of many who held court at the café, it is his insouciant style – and literary works, of course – that resounds. Here he is seen perfectly accessorized with a Leftist protest paper.

As star of seminal films such as *The Philadelphia Story* (1940), *North by Northwest* (1959) and *Charade* (1963), British-born actor Cary Grant (1904–86), originally Archibald Alexander Leach, is the ultimate Hollywood leading man. On screen, he drifted between comedic and dramatic roles, almost always playing a well-dressed, refined man of wealth and substance. Off screen, he was Hollywood royalty: his impressively long career, stretching from around 1937 to 1963, meant that he became one of the industry's wealthiest performers, enjoying a strong box-office record for his near-30-year reign.

Grant continues to be an influential figure in terms of style, and his personal look a touchstone for contemporary designers such as Giorgio Armani and Michael Kors. The actor's sophisticated image was underpinned by perfectly cut suiting – double-breasted jackets, worsted-wool jackets and scarves, Savile Row suits – his silhouette slimming down to a contemporary, modish look in the late 1950s and early 1960s.

Grant did not seem to follow trends, or consider himself to be particularly fashionable, wearing a mix of ready-made suiting and bespoke or tailored pieces that were put together with a real eye for practicality. He understood the power of clothing to streamline the silhouette, and held dear the advice of his father that it was better to own one good pair of shoes than four cheap ones. He also found it a little ostentatious to show off a monogrammed handkerchief in the chest pocket.

British actor Cary Grant is seen here leaving his London hotel in April 1946, during a rare excursion from Hollywood. In what must be the world's politest paparazzo shot, Grant appears to be just as refined off screen as he is on screen – dark wool suiting and a double-breasted overcoat provide a powerful and dignified silhouette.

TRUMAN CAPOTE

American writer Truman Capote (1924–84) enjoyed a celebrity and success so rarely achieved in the world of literature. Capote wrote short stories, novels, plays and screenplays, articles and profiles, and enjoyed friendships with many well-known people, from Marilyn Monroe to Andy Warhol. The literary high point of his career may be the 'non-fiction novel' *In Cold Blood* (1965), a work created with the help of Capote's friend, author Harper Lee, but his best-known work is the novella *Breakfast at Tiffany's* (1958), perhaps because of its 1961 cinematic reworking starring Audrey Hepburn.

Two portraits of the author helped kick-start Capote's career as an *enfant terrible*. Harold Halma's 1947 photograph of the young fire-eyed Louisianan used on the back of the writer's debut bestseller, *Other Voices, Other Rooms* (1948), marked out the young talent as a somewhat dangerous creative. Carl Van Vechten's 1948 portrait of Capote in a striped T-shirt against a backdrop of marionettes pushed the idea of the writer as a controversial, whimsical waif. His openness about his homosexuality shocked some, and there was often a mannered defiance in Capote's personal style. Alongside trim suits and crystal-framed tinted-lens eyewear, there would often be a touch of the flamboyant: an impossibly long striped scarf, a floppy fedora, a natty bow tie or a pair of turquoise trousers. Appearing on television talk shows later in life, Capote is a deliciously dark and charismatic storyteller, waspish and mischievous, and always impeccably dressed.

Carl Van Vechten's 1948 studio portrait (the shot was to be Capote's official dust-jacket photograph) shows the young author caught between two worlds: he is both an adult and a bored child surrounded by his toys. His simple striped T-shirt, rather than a shirt and tie, marked him out as a man who would do things a little differently.

The writer in 1980, four years before his death, dressed down in a cotton shirt and denim jeans. A touch of whimsy was a key element in Capote's personal style, both in terms of pose and accessories, which here include a jaunty oxblood fedora and a fan.

JAMES DEAN

American actor James Dean (1931–55) was 24 years old when he was killed in a car crash near Cholane, California. His iconic status is remarkable, particularly as his creative output encompasses only three films in which he took a starring role. *East of Eden* (1955), *Rebel Without a Cause* (1955) and *Giant* (1956) are the cinematic classics that punctuated Dean's career, but his rumoured off-screen liaisons, bad-boy style and tragically early death have ensured that his fame has endured.

In 1955, the year that arguably saw the birth of teen culture, Dean was cast in *Rebel* as Jim Stark, the troubled outsider, the young man struggling with rage and an inner darkness, dressed in impossibly cool outfits. As Jim, he wore a bright-red Harrington jacket, classic white T-shirt and dark-indigo Lee jeans, which became the unofficial uniform for a generation of teenagers wanting to look different from their parents. *East of Eden* saw Dean as Cal Trask, dressed in preppy sun-faded knits and shirts, and as ranch hand Jett Rink in *Giant* he wore beautifully bashed-up denim.

If images of the on-screen Dean provided defining moments in cinema, it was the young actor's off-screen looks that have become evergreen references for modern men. Inspired somewhat by Marlon Brando, photographs of Dean in a simple Breton top, a dark worn-down pea coat, tortoiseshell glasses and a messy pompadour hairstyle remain the touchstones of contemporary men's style.

James Dean wore a dishevelled, eclectic look on and off screen that seemed to communicate a rejection of societal norms. He rarely looked like a moneyed movie star, and more like an artist struggling with the attention that came with his burgeoning celebrity. This shot from the 1950s makes much of Dean's rough-edged teen-rebel look.

MARLON BRANDO

All bulges and brawn in *A Streetcar Named Desire* (the classic 1951 film that cemented his stardom), and grease-smudged in *The Wild One* (1953), legendary actor and director Marlon Brando (1924–2004) unwittingly made the simple T-shirt the epitome of manliness. Brando's early on-screen style – downbeat, blue-collar, real – pieced together with simple workwear garments, worn-in denim and leather, coined an enduring and timeless look. The T-shirt remains a staple of every man's wardrobe, and classic workwear brands dominate contemporary men's fashion.

Two Academy Awards – almost 20 years apart – were high points in a volatile career that spanned four decades; award nominations for *A Streetcar Named Desire*, *Julius Caesar* (1953) and *Sayonara* (1957) laid the way for a win for Francis Ford Coppola's *The Godfather* (1972) and a nomination for the erotic drama *Last Tango in Paris* (1972). With a reputation for being difficult to work with, Brando channelled his off-screen rebelliousness into his advocacy for civil rights. In 1973, on live television, he chose not to accept his Oscar for *The Godfather*, instead giving the platform to an Apache woman, Sacheen Littlefeather, in protest of the treatment of indigenous Americans by the film industry – to a chorus of cheering and booing.

Brando's performance as gang leader Johnny Strabler in *The Wild One* is perhaps his most enduring image, both tough and authentic but also highly fetishized: the Perfecto leather jacket (later favoured by Johnny Ramone), tilted peaked cap, jeans, sideburns and sunglasses, and the classic T-shirt. Brando's own gleaming 1950 Triumph Thunderbird 6T motorcycle is the ultimate man's accessory.

Brando in the 1950s, eschewing the Hollywood tradition of slickly suited male lead actors with his casual, downbeat – almost unkempt – look. Even when dressed in loose, mismatched suiting, as he is here, his look would often underline a rebellious attitude.

The 1953 publicity portrait issued for *The Wild One*, with Brando as muscle-bound biker Johnny Strabler – a look that continues to inspire fashion design and fetish wear alike.

PABLO PICASSO

1955

Pablo Picasso (1881–1973), one of the world's greatest artists, is known for his ground-breaking paintings, prints and sculptures … and for his lifelong love of Breton stripes. For most of his photographic portraits, Picasso clung to the easy cool of the striped T-shirt – or simply elected to wear no shirt at all.

From his precocious beginnings at the School of Fine Arts in Barcelona and Madrid's Royal Academy of San Fernando, Picasso went on to work in a wealth of visual styles. With his relocation to Paris in the early 1900s, his Blue Period light-footed through a world of weeping women and beggars. Later came Cubism and Surrealism, creating a capricious portfolio of classical modernist paintings, scratchy cartoonish portraits and gnarled bronze casts.

Picasso spent most of his working life in the south of France, perhaps explaining his Gallic-inspired personal style. A series of muscular self-portraits created throughout his life show a vital man in simple dress, larger than life, but the artist's later years saw him add a jaunty flat cap or scarf and beret to his look, almost always with his famous striped T-shirt.

The ultimate laid-back dresser, after his college days – when he wore his jet-black hair slightly long – Picasso settled comfortably into an artfully dishevelled, utilitarian look, largely comprising crumpled worker jackets, baggy trench coats and plaid flannel shirting. Photographs taken in the years preceding his death show a tanned older man playing with his dachshunds, or working in his studio, resplendent in a pair of well-worn shorts and scuffed leather slippers.

A portrait of the Spanish painter in September 1955 by photographer George Stroud. In his later years, Picasso favoured a uniform of sorts, overlooking contemporary style in favour of a simple, pared-down look with a touch of rakish humour. Breton-striped shirts were his go-to, and today they remain a shortcut to cool.

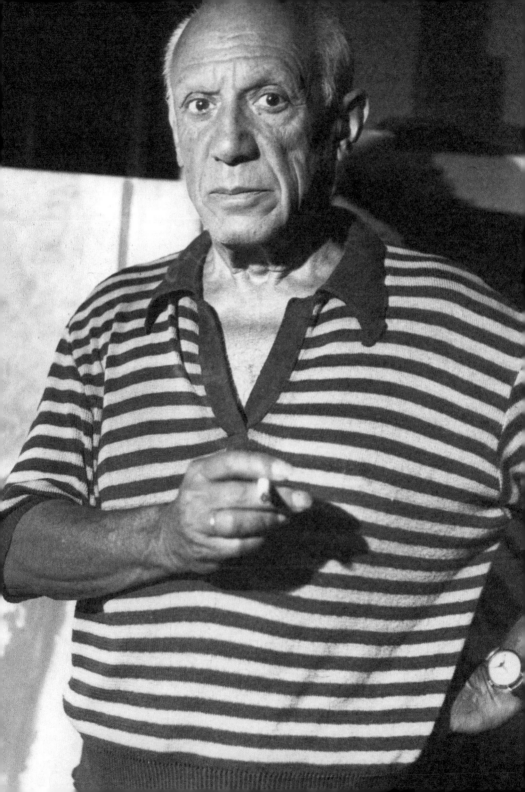

JACK KEROUAC

1959

Ultimate American anti-hero, Jack Kerouac (1922–69) was the handsome cult writer whose spontaneous prose defined the Beat movement. Kerouac's free-form literary style was informed by the jazz of Charlie Parker and Dizzy Gillespie, Buddhism (Kerouac wrote a biography of Siddhartha Gautama, published posthumously) and drug-induced epiphanies.

Kerouac's contemporaries Allen Ginsberg and William S Burroughs and other creative friends drifted in and out of his books, as did his real-life experiences, from booze and sex to Catholicism. Kerouac's mediocre early career was transformed when the publication of *On the Road* (1957) – his meandering, visceral travelogue of two road-tripping friends – brought the writer sudden celebrity.

In many ways, Kerouac's personal style was traditionally all-American: he wore simple T-shirts and plaid shirts, loose-cut khakis, worker and chore jackets, and tough, selvage denim in classic rich indigo, the unofficial uniform of blue-collar workers and drifters for hire. Workwear is an especially hardy style genre – it has moved through more than 125 years of history and remained intact. Its practicality, authenticity and implied aestheticism obviously appealed to Kerouac, and his look – powered by his controversial literary infamy – has endured.

This 1959 portrait by John Cohen of Kerouac and his contemporary Allen Ginsberg – apparently in deep, bookish discussion – shows the Beat writers' penchant for American workwear outfits. Brushed plaid shirting, khakis, worker jackets and indigo-dyed denim are classic menswear pieces that are still in beat with contemporary style.

SAMMY DAVIS JR

The first African-American man to be featured on the cover of *GQ* in 1967 (in a skinny double-breasted grey plaid suit), Sammy Davis Jr (1925–90) was an all-singing, all-dancing, award-winning entertainer who appeared in more than 40 feature films, musicals and plays.

Davis had been a child star, dancing in a trio with his father and a family friend, Will Mastin, a vaudeville performer, and then became a nightclub crooner after military service. His 1951 Academy Awards after-party performance at Ciro's in West Hollywood put Davis in the sights of the celebrity elite, and in 1960 Davis starred in his first Rat Pack film, *Ocean's 11*.

Davis's father had shielded him from racial prejudice as a child, but as an adult even his celebrity status could not protect him from it. As headliner at a casino in Las Vegas, Davis – like other black performers – had to go without a dressing room, and he was not able to stay in the hotels in which he performed, or even dine in them. Later, he would refuse to play venues that segregated their acts.

There are many iconic images of Davis: off duty with Frank Sinatra and Dean Martin, performing on *The Sammy Davis Jr. Show* (1966) or lounging backstage in smoky dressing rooms, wearing a pinstripe suit, white shirt and loosened slim black tie. In the late 1970s his look became as flamboyant as the age dictated, but he perhaps looked best in his Rat Pack heyday in the early 1960s, slick and suited, yet loose and louche.

Light on his feet, the *Ocean's 11* star Sammy Davis Jr does what he did best in this energetic action shot from 1959 – with perfectly matched vest and socks. Davis's physical prowess as a dancer was the result of years as a young vaudeville performer and he continued to tap-dance late into his career.

By 1960 Sammy Davis Jr had appeared in more than eight major movies, been nominated for an Emmy Award and scored a star on the Hollywood Walk of Fame. His style was unapologetically slick and laid-back, featuring double-breasted suiting, open-neck shirt and cravat.

TERENCE STAMP

In the mid-1960s, when Swinging London was the centre of the creative world, actor Terence Stamp (1938–) was at its heart. A rare coming together of upper- and working-class Londoners saw a creative explosion of music, art and fashion. As the gangly-limbed son of a tugboat worker, with coal-black hair and ice-blue eyes, Stamp became the embodiment of this new, seemingly classless and cultured youth.

Peter Ustinov's film *Billy Budd* (Stamp's 1962 cinematic debut) and John Schlesinger's *Far from the Madding Crowd* (1967) marked Stamp out as a dreamy matinée idol, before Ken Loach's *Poor Cow* (1967) played on the young actor's rougher, East End edge. But it was his romances with Julie Christie and Jean Shrimpton, and a blind date with Brigitte Bardot, that made Stamp a household name. His relationship with Jean Shrimpton was documented obsessively, the pair posing together in countless photoshoots, dressed to the nines.

Inspired by his father, Stamp had an obsession with sharp suits, made-to-measure by 'Fred the Stitch', the tailor Douglas Hayward, from his Mayfair shop; bespoke leather shoes; and the occasional hat. As the decade progressed and Stamp's fame grew, so did his fashion choices. He became bolder, more confident, and, apart from almost nine years living in India, his perfectly cut style remained intact, with one concession: he was less likely to be wearing his favourite handmade shoes than Birkenstocks with white socks.

The British actor – young, waif-like and dishevelled – relaxing in a London bar in the 1960s. (Spot his contemporary and one-time flatmate Michael Caine in the background.) Although Stamp's personal style developed into real sartorial perfection, there is something timeless about this laid-back look from his youth.

The poster for Ken Loach's *Poor Cow* (1967), a film adapted from Nell Dunn's ground-breaking book. Stamp played sensitive criminal Dave Fuller with bohemian aplomb, in a chunky roll-neck sweater, denim shirt and suede boots.

JOHN F KENNEDY

After the suffocating conservatism of the 1950s, the 35th President of the United States, John Fitzgerald Kennedy (1917–63), was the embodiment of youth and optimism. The rich, successful playboy with a social conscience was a member of the Kennedy clan, the sun-kissed all-American family that had near-royal status. It follows that his personal style was less European and – excitingly – more obviously American. With a core wardrobe of crumpled shirting and chunky crew-neck knits, 'JFK' dealt in the laid-back chic of mismatched suiting, chinos and tennis shoes, easy wool sports jackets and cool tortoiseshell shades.

In a conscious step away from the formalities of past political reporting, photographers followed Kennedy and his family behind the scenes, creating a loose, reportage-style document of their lives. On securing the presidency in January 1961, Kennedy moved into the White House with his young family, and his wife Jackie Kennedy restored and revamped the interiors in a symbolic gesture that signalled a new age.

Much has been written about Kennedy's timeless style: the Ivy League preppiness, the break from presidential tradition in his off-duty style, and the implied power of Brooks Brothers suiting in grey or blue, sometimes styled with the sliver of a white pocket square peaking out. On the campaign trail he wore a monogrammed shirt; at formal events he wore slim-fitting dinner suits; and he was photographed in a silk top hat and morning suit, bringing a sense of cool to the refined but staid look. Iconic images of Kennedy at the podium endure, but informal portraits of the man sailing, eating an ice cream, enjoying life with his family, resound the most.

At the podium John F Kennedy was the ultimate power dresser, but it was his off-duty laid-back look that marked him out as a true icon of style. Behind the scenes he was a family man who dressed down in perfectly preppy outfits, seen here in a sports jacket, pale chinos and dark tortoiseshell sunglasses in April 1963, some eight months before his assassination.

SEAN CONNERY

In 1951 a young Sean Connery (1930–), dressed in a small pair of swim shorts, was a Mr Universe finalist, arguably the lauded actor's first theatrical performance. A lifeguard, life model and footballer, Connery also worked backstage at the King's Theatre in Edinburgh and joined an English production of *South Pacific* in 1953. Other minor stage roles followed, then roles on television and in film, but his career highlight is his portrayal of a British secret agent, kick-starting a multimillion-dollar film franchise. Connery played James Bond for the first five films in the series, from 1962 to 1967, and then again in 1971 and 1983.

Connery's seven Bond films helped mark him out as one of the world's best-dressed men. Borrowing a little from the series' suave protagonist, his personal style became entwined with his on-screen persona. Bond's perfectly cut casual suiting (slim, 1960s-influenced), Savile Row dinner jackets and tweed sports jackets, refined knits and upscale leisurewear became Connery's go-to look.

Off screen, there is a touch of whimsy to the actor's early portraits. He seems naturally handsome, well built, rugged even, but always completely at ease with his surroundings. He is pictured around countless dinner tables, laughing with famous actors, lounging on sofas or messily eating spaghetti – there is an easy physicality to Connery that underpins his personal style.

This official United Artists portrait of Sean Connery from 1964 shows the actor in character as James Bond, in the mountains with his Aston Martin DB5, in a scene from *Goldfinger*. Connery's style – encapsulated in perfectly cut suiting – was informed by the slick costume design for Bond, a character the actor made his own.

BOB DYLAN

1965

Bob Dylan (1941–) is the American cult musician whose politically engaged output – from 'Blowin' in the Wind' to 'The Times They Are a-Changin'' – became the soundtrack to the 1960s and 1970s counterculture movement. Against a backdrop of anti-war demonstrations, civil rights marches, and a growing tension between the conservative old guard and disillusioned youth, Dylan's work often eschewed pop and rock's obsession with love and addressed real issues.

Born Robert Zimmerman, Dylan held steadfast to his look throughout the 1960s, 1970s and beyond: big hair, crumpled shirting, skinny jeans and battered overcoats. Early days saw him wear dark blazers with scaled-down lapels over a striped T-shirt, the occasional polka-dot shirt or, often, a black turtleneck sweater.

As his music evolved from acoustic to electric (the 1965 album *Bringing It All Back Home* was his first using electric instruments), his lyrics also became more experimental. His style upgraded, too, with dark glasses, pointed Chelsea boots (sometimes with Cuban heels), striped blazers, but always with his wild, unkempt hair.

Now in his later years, Dylan continues to perform. His on-stage style is punctuated with wide-brimmed hats, Western shirts and bootlace ties.

The young artist in 1965 with his trademark big hair and a simple striped T-shirt. Apart from a Swinging Sixties upgrade, Dylan's look remained constant throughout his early career.

May 1966 and Dylan's style had changed; his 1965 album *Bringing it All Back Home* used electric instruments and his clothing had evolved to reflect a London-influenced look.

BOBBY SEALE

Bobby Seale (1936–) is the American political activist who railed against the institutional and overt racism of the mid-1960s and 1970s.

The assassination of American Muslim minister Malcolm X in 1965, a turning point in American racial politics, inspired Seale and friend Huey Newton to create the Black Panther Party in 1966. In the face of police brutality and unchallenged racism, Seale and Newton's new party caught fire. They adopted Malcolm X's modus operandi – 'Freedom by any means necessary' – and embraced an uneasy relationship with violence. Initially, the Black Panthers operated armed citizen patrols to counter police brutality, but by 1969 the movement had expanded into community projects, such as the Free Breakfast for Children Program and health centres. FBI head J Edgar Hoover is rumoured to have described the party as the greatest threat to the internal security of the United States.

Seale's persona as chairman of the party is a lesson in political power dressing. Slick camel overcoats, big-collar shirts and ties marked him as a formidable politician. His black beret, worn at an angle, military-style, and a black-leather single-breasted jacket with a badge on the lapel, over a roll-neck sweater or shirt, became the Panthers' tough-edged uniform.

Through Seale, Panther iconography grew in popularity: at the 1968 Olympics, two American medallists gave the Panthers' 'black power' salute from the winners' podium (and were banned by the International Olympic Committee for life); celebrities from American actress Jane Fonda to French writer Jean Genet were supporters. Seale's legacy is real social change and an enduring political movement where visibility is key.

Black Panther activist Bobby Seale at work in the late 1960s. His personal look – featuring leather jacket and roll-neck sweater – became a much-copied expression of dissent in a political movement that harnessed the power of style.

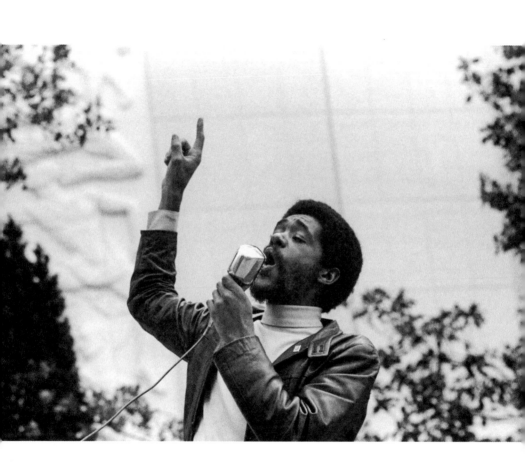

STEVE McQUEEN

Motorbikes, movies and the easy effortlessness of a Harrington jacket, worn-in denim and a simple T-shirt, bound up in a confident, authentic masculinity: Steve McQueen (1930–80) was the king of cool, an actor with natural talent and good looks, whose relaxed, off-duty attitude belied a troubled past. He looked great in almost anything, but it is his smart-casual style that endures, chiming perfectly with the ideal of modern men's dressing: relaxed, unfussy, with a hint of heritage.

A youth of petty crime, teenage rebellion and family violence saw McQueen join the United States Marine Corps in 1947. Having been honourably discharged in 1950, he began studying acting in 1952, part-funded by weekend motorcycle races at Long Island City Raceway. His breakout roles were in television Westerns and the Frank Sinatra film *Never So Few* (1959). His most famous films, arguably *The Great Escape* (1963), *Bullitt* (1968) and the physically gruelling *Papillion* (1973), made him one of the world's most influential movie stars, until his death in 1980.

McQueen remains the go-to reference for contemporary designers and stylists; his laid-back, preppy look has inspired a distinct, if not commercial, genre of men's style. In fine knits and button-down shirts, McQueen could almost have been dressed by J Crew. British heritage brand Barbour has based pieces on his style, and McQueen's raglan-sleeve sweats and beaten-up leather jackets are the hipster uniform around the world. So powerful is McQueen's enduring image that his estate is one of the highest earning of deceased celebrities in the world.

Was there ever a man cooler than Steve McQueen? The actor's enduring look is captured perfectly here in this portrait from the 1960s. In a white, weather-worn T-shirt and slim, pale chinos – dark glasses in hand – his outfit could be 100-per-cent contemporary.

Steve McQueen lived fast, taking on physically challenging roles, and motorbike racing was his passion. Pale workwear trousers and a simple, heavyweight sweatshirt provided the outfit in which to do it.

ANDY WARHOL 1969

The bewigged American artist at the epicentre of the Pop art movement, Andy Warhol (1928–87) was a shy, unassuming Pennsylvanian who presided over a coterie of legendary creatives, musicians, models, celebrities, drag queens and oddballs in 1960s, 1970s and 1980s New York.

Well-known portraits of Warhol show him in a black polo-neck sweater, Breton top or natty shirt and tie, one or more near-identical brittle platinum wigs and crystal-framed eyewear. His look was his trademark, a pared-down style that, although it had a hint of eccentricity, was in stark contrast to the colourful characters that hung out at The Factory, Warhol's aluminium-lined and sliver-painted studio.

Many lives intersected at The Factory. It became the meeting place of intellectuals and artists, musicians such as Debbie Harry, David Bowie, Bob Dylan, Lou Reed and Mick Jagger, writers including Truman Capote and William S Burroughs, and fashion designers such as Halston, along with Warhol's bohemian friends and 'superstars' Candy Darling, Holly Woodlawn and Joe Dallesandro. Most of these figures are now celebrated in their chosen discipline.

In 1968 Warhol survived a murder attempt that left him with lifelong medical problems. The Factory increased security, marking something of an end to the creative freedom the Warhol set had enjoyed for almost a decade. In the 1970s and early 1980s Warhol began to secure high-fee portrait commissions, and received vast sums of money as well as criticism for the way he balanced art and commerce. His legacy is a collection of films, drawings, screen prints and sculptures, *Interview* magazine, The Velvet Underground, album covers, books and approximately 600 time capsules – boxed and filed letters, objects and ephemera – and 30 silver-white wigs.

The artist in 1969 wearing a striped T-shirt and glossy black-leather biker jacket: Warhol's typically pared-down look remains shorthand for cool.

A film still of Warhol from the early 1980s in a bohemian turtleneck sweater and spiky platinum wig.

46

MICK JAGGER

In his youth, Mick Jagger (1943–) was a fragile-looking, long-haired waif, dressed in delicate florals, theatrical furs and impossibly tight jeans, who transformed on stage into a sinewy, sexualized performer, full of visceral energy. As the front man of The Rolling Stones, the British supergroup, Jagger is considered one of the world's most influential musicians and distinctive male style icons.

In 1961 Jagger shared an apartment in Chelsea with an old school friend, Keith Richards, and soon set up a band with guitarist Brian Jones. In 1962 they played their first major gig at London's Marquee Club. The decade belonged to men like Jagger. The crushing of traditional societal norms, a revolution of attitudes towards sex and a focus on pop culture meant that working-class kids like Jagger could use creativity to become socially mobile. Jagger's talent as a musician was matched by his position at the epicentre of a new kind of men's style. Through his personal look – comparable with that of David Bowie, his friend – the skinny-limbed performer played with ideas of luxury, raw sexuality and gender fluidity.

Images of Jagger with his partners, wife Bianca Pérez-Mora Macias, then Jerry Hall, show a wealth of experimental outfits, but the photographs that document his relationship with fellow musician Marianne Faithfull (from 1966 to 1970) mark the pair out as a couple who seemed to embody the spirit of the decade. Jagger wore ruffles and furs, loud suits and velvet jackets, a rock-edged London look that resounds to this day.

Charting the evolution of Mick Jagger's personal style is to follow the progression of British fashion in the 1960s and 1970s, a time when creativity was unleashed. This perfectly constructed image shows the musician playing the part of a colonial gentleman reclining on a chaise, his famous pout in the shadow of an extravagant Panama hat.

The export of British style into a different culture seems only to underline its distinctiveness. Here, Jagger rehearses for *The Ed Sullivan Show* in New York in November 1969. (Spot Keith Richards in the background.)

DAVID BOWIE

In the early 1970s, a dismal period in the UK, David Bowie (born David Jones; 1947–2016) was a ginger-haired oddity who braved the streets of London in a dress. The ground-breaking pop-music and fashion artist cut a path through the mainstream, blurring the boundaries between musical and fashion genres, and toying with an ambiguous gender and sexuality. Soon, everyone wanted to be just like him, his notoriously obsessive fans copying his costumes, hair and make-up as well as his sheer bravado – such was the sway of Bowie's star power.

Throughout his career Bowie created performance personae that informed his music, style and album artwork. Ziggy Stardust, Aladdin Sane and the Thin White Duke were the characters who dominated Bowie's output, but he created others, too. Growing up in the London suburb of Beckenham, he was first a clean-cut mod and then a curly-haired Free Festival hippie. Bowie capriciously stole ideas and references, taking old ideas and making them new again; his on-stage look for the Ziggy Stardust Tour (1972–3) was influenced by the ancient tradition of kabuki, reworked by Japanese designer Kansai Yamamoto, who created many of Bowie's stage outfits. In Nicolas Roeg's *The Man Who Fell to Earth* (1976) he played a homeless alien with flame-red hair, white T-shirt and trench coat with upturned collar, and in Jim Henson's *Labyrinth* (1986) he appeared as sprightly goblin royalty, in leather, sequins, frilled shirts and tights.

At the end of his life, days after his 69th birthday and the release of his farewell album, *Blackstar* (2016), a final photograph of Bowie was released. He is pictured on a New York street in a wide-brimmed hat and slim dark-grey suit, white shirt and grey tie, wearing black leather shoes, no socks and a grin.

Bowie's live performances were electric, each an energetic portmanteau of avant-garde fashion, mystifying performance art and good old-fashioned rock and roll. This image, taken at the Hammersmith Odeon, London, in 1973, shows Bowie as Ziggy Stardust, flipping about the stage in one of Kansai Yamamoto's asymmetric stage outfits.

Munich, 1976. Although Bowie is off duty, he is seemingly still in character: his own slick sci-fi version of the English gentlemanly style, in thick wool tweed, 1970s flares and future-focused sunglasses.

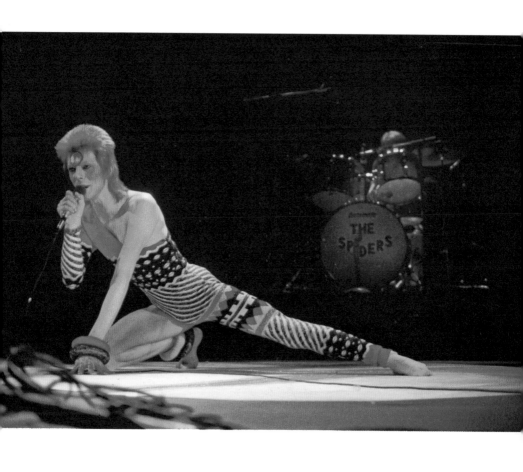

Mink coats, wide-brimmed hats, 1930s gangster suits and a pumped-up Rolls-Royce: Walt 'Clyde' Frazier (1945–) is the New York Knicks basketball star from Atlanta, Georgia. Known for his style, both on and off the court, Frazier famously led the Knicks to win their only two NBA (National Basketball Association) championship titles in 1970 and 1973.

As a rookie young player in New York, Frazier was influenced both by a lineage of outlandishly dressed sports stars and the upbeat street style of late-1960s Harlem. He started to wear an Italian Borsalino hat with a wide brim (at odds with the fashion for narrow-brimmed headwear at the time). He endured laughter from his team-mates until Arthur Penn's *Bonnie and Clyde* (1967) was released a few weeks later. Clyde, played by Warren Beatty, wore a similar hat and Frazier found himself ahead of the curve – earning himself the nickname 'Clyde'.

Sports fans loved Frazier's off-court antics and his loud, trend-breaking outfits; after Chuck Taylor and his association with Converse All-Stars in 1932, Frazier was the first basketball star to collaborate on a sneaker, the Puma Clyde.

One iconic shot of Frazier shows him in a dark, refined turtleneck with a gold pendant on a long chain, a wide-brimmed hat and a rather theatrical studded leather-trimmed cape. Others show him in plaid, pinstripe suiting, slim-fitting with graceful flares: the perfect 1970s silhouette.

Although Walt Frazier's successful sports career had allowed him to enjoy the finer things in life – including a $20,000 Rolls-Royce – he is pictured here taking the subway to work in April 1974, wearing one of his trademark outfits with a wide-brimmed hat.

ROBERT REDFORD

Robert Redford (1936–) is Hollywood's handsome leading man, an actor, director and activist, founder of the Sundance Film Festival, and *Time* magazine's 'godfather of indie film'. Redford's muscular activism and lifelong support of independent film-making mark him out as a singular, progressive artist. This headstrong quality is reflected in his personal style: there is an easy functionality to it, as if he is the man who gets things done – and just happens to look great in the process.

Key films mark Redford's style: he is super-slick as Jay Gatsby in Jack Clayton's *The Great Gatsby* (1974), and wears beaten-up Western outfits and an all-black suit topped with a black wide-brimmed hat in George Roy Hill's *Butch Cassidy and the Sundance Kid* (1969). In Sydney Pollack's *Three Days of the Condor* (1975) he wears a pale-blue cambric shirt, dark crew-neck sweater, tweed jacket and jeans, a preppy look that could almost be contemporary.

In the 1970s Redford lived between Hollywood, New York and his newly acquired Utah ski resort on the east side of Mount Timpanogos, which the actor renamed Sundance. The area suited Redford's outdoorsy bent – he skis and climbs – and photographs of the actor from this period are a balance of powerful suiting, oversized collars and ties, and a rugged, off-duty athleticism typified by flannel plaid shirts, gilet and denim jacket.

This shot of Robert Redford taken in 1976 shows an athletic, easy-going confidence – the foundation of the sense of style for which he became known. Although this outfit – flared denim jeans, denim panelled jacket and baker-boy cap – is obviously from the 1970s, underlying it is a subtle workwear practicality that informs how Redford dresses to this day.

JOHN LYDON

Under the snarling, orange-haired guise of 'Johnny Rotten', John Lydon (1956–) was the lead singer of the Sex Pistols and post-punk outfit Public Image Ltd. He swore on television, insulted the Queen, and chose a stage surname that was a nod to his bad dental hygiene.

Lydon spent his childhood in North London and left home after he was ordered to cut his long hair, only then to crop it short and dye it bright green. In 1975 music manager Malcolm McLaren – co-owner, with Vivienne Westwood, of London fashion boutique SEX – sought to put together a new band to rival US punk outfit New York Dolls. Lydon, who had been hanging out at SEX, was chosen as the band's front man, less for his vocal talents and more for his angry attitude and rough-edged look. Although the band stayed together only just long enough to record one album and four singles, they became the beating heart of the British punk scene in the late 1970s.

In Lydon, McLaren had found a vehicle for a burgeoning music and art movement that stood in opposition to mainstream 1970s Britain, a leader of a rebellious youth that DIYed their clothing and accessorized it with spiked hair, safety pins and garbage bags. Powered by street style rather than fashion, Lydon, his band mates and followers of the wider punk scene wore bright-red Royal Stewart tartan shot through with rips, doctored T-shirts and Westwood's infamous bondage trousers.

In 1976 John Lydon was Johnny Rotten, the gangly, flame-haired troublemaker firmly at the front of the British punk movement. Unlike its American counterpart, the British punk scene was – in part – powered by style, art and creativity. Here, Lydon's outfit is DIYed with the accents of punk style – zips, studs and safety pins.

JOHNNY RAMONE

Distressed skinny jeans, T-shirts, leather jackets and tennis shoes: Johnny Ramone (1948–2004), the goofy, angry punk guitarist from Queens, New York, helped develop a deceptively simple look that went on to underwrite a whole genre of contemporary style.

As a young musician in 1970s New York, the working-class military-academy graduate's clever instinct was that his punk rock band, the Ramones, should have a look that was almost as important as the music, if not more so. His personal style had been a steady progression from velvet suits and snakeskin shoes to denim jackets (with no shirt) and tie-dye headbands. As the band developed, Ramone experimented with its members' clothes, driving them towards a shamelessly glitter-edged style with silver lamé and black spandex. Finally, the band evolved into jeans, T-shirts and long hair, Perfecto leather jackets and Keds or Converse sneakers, a perfectly judged style that would strike a chord with their young, alternative fan base.

Drawing influence from The Stooges, the Ramones had an indelible influence on punk music and culture in the US and UK. By the time of its debut at New York's historic CBGB venue in 1974, the band's unique look had become the go-to uniform for punk's devotees. Under Johnny's stewardship, the Ramones embodied an angry authenticity, and its visual style remains a touchstone for modern designers, stylists and anyone wanting to add a pinch of measured rebellion into their wardrobe. Today, many of the wearers of Johnny Ramone's look might not be aware of the true origin of their style – the experimentations of an angry young man from Queens who would make a point to scowl at the camera whenever his picture was taken.

Johnny Ramone on stage and in action at the Roundhouse, London, in July 1976. As the mastermind behind the Ramones' image, evolving it from glam rock to an easy-to-copy indie look, Johnny Ramone coined a style that has endured like no other.

BRUCE SPRINGSTEEN 1978

Known affectionately as 'The Boss', the musician, singer-songwriter and political activist Bruce Springsteen (1949–) deals in the American Dream. Through his music, Springsteen creates a fantasy landscape of sparking steelworks, trailer parks and lumberyards; his songs are paeans to honest American families that are trying to make their way in the world.

Springsteen's personal style follows suit. In his early years he wore simple, quintessentially American clothing – leather biker jackets, pea coats and plaid shirts – with long, tousled hair. On the cover of his 1984 album, *Born in the USA*, Springsteen wore the ultimate American rock outfit: a white T-shirt, a pair of wonderfully worn denim jeans and a bandana. Known for his energetic live performances and political advocacy, Springsteen's style has matured of late, but he still holds on to the easy functionality and downbeat romance of American workwear.

Springsteen's lyrical poeticism, narrative style, blue-collar realism and upbeat rock edge have made him a multimillion-dollar industry, and on or off stage his authentic, rough-edged style underlines an impressive physicality. This unapologetically tough, masculine way of dressing has made him a mainstream and much-loved all-American hero.

An iconic portrait of Springsteen by lauded British photographer Terry O'Neill.

The 26-year-old Springsteen performing live at Red Bank, New Jersey on the *Born To Run* tour, October 1975. He started the set in his unofficial uniform: boot cut jeans, a battered leather biker jacket and braces – and ended it sweaty and smiling in an unbuttoned white shirt.

IAN CURTIS

Ian Curtis (1956–80) was the British singer-songwriter and front man of Joy Division who committed suicide in 1980 on the eve of the band's first American tour.

Curtis had sharp features with coal-black eyes and messy black hair; he, dressed simply, in crumpled shirts with the sleeves carefully folded up, suit trousers or jeans, leather shoes and his trademark trench coat. The look of the band was integral to the music: its members eschewed the showy anarchy of punk and favoured a pared-down, anti-fashion approach. The cover of Joy Division's *Unknown Pleasures* album, released in 1979, is by legendary graphic artist Peter Saville: a simple monochromatic wave pattern that is as iconic as Curtis himself.

Joy Division formed in Salford, Greater Manchester, in 1976 – Curtis had met keyboard-player Bernard Sumner at a Sex Pistols gig – and is considered one of the founding bands of the post-punk movement. Curtis's early musical idols were David Bowie and Iggy Pop (although he borrowed little, if nothing, from the two musicians' approaches to style). He was influenced by poetry and literature, and he tried to balance life as a burgeoning star with the pressures of being a young father. Curtis struggled with epilepsy and depression and, as Joy Division's popularity grew, the musician found live performances increasingly difficult. Had he lived, Curtis would have had to endure an even greater success: 'Love Will Tear Us Apart', Joy Division's most enduring and popular song, was due to be released just two weeks after Curtis's death.

Joy Division front man Ian Curtis performing in March 1979 at the Bowden Vale Youth Club in south Manchester. At odds with the style-heavy industries of punk and pop, Curtis and the band affected an anti-fashion stance but – paradoxically – his crumpled shirts and charity-shop slacks became indescribably cool.

FREDDIE MERCURY

Known for his perfectly clipped moustache, toothy grin and passionate vocal performances, Freddie Mercury (born Farrokh Bulsara; 1946–91) was the singer, songwriter, producer and flamboyant front man of legendary rock band Queen. Mercury spent his childhood in Tanzania and India, his musical talent obvious from an early age. Having moved with his family to the UK in 1964, in his early twenties Mercury performed with a couple of ailing bands and sold vintage clothes at London's Kensington Market, but then joined fellow musicians Brian May and Roger Taylor to form Queen in 1970.

Penning and performing some of the world's most influential pop and rock songs, Mercury brought together the odd bedfellows of muscular rock and theatrical camp. He wrote Queen's biggest hits, including 'Killer Queen' (1974), 'Don't Stop Me Now' (1979) and the experimental 'Bohemian Rhapsody' (1975). On stage he wore sequined one-pieces, cut low to bare his chest, impossibly tight tights and slick leather; he played with the pomp of military dress and drew from the gay fetish scene with Aviators, white vests, denim and studded bicep bands.

Much has been written on Mercury's stagecraft, which often left his fans – and his peers – in awe. His performance with Queen at Live Aid in 1985, in front of 72,000 fans, is thought of as *the* landmark rock performance. His exuberance on stage belied his apparently shy off-stage persona.

In this image from 1982 Freddie Mercury – at the height of his fame – gets his trademark moustache trimmed. On stage or on set, Mercury would appear to be unbelievably confident; his personal style was daring and highly sexualized, drawing cues from the fetish scene, military dress and macho iconography.

Mercury – performing his signature fist punch – on stage with Queen at Live Aid in 1985.

BRYAN FERRY

The English fashion designer Antony Price is best known for his legendary image-making skills. Under his guidance, fledgling pop and rock musicians became international stars, notably David Bowie and the members of Duran Duran, but it was Price's work with Roxy Music that made its front man, Bryan Ferry (1945–), the most stylish man in pop.

Ferry's style influenced a whole generation, an unlikely outcome for a working-class pottery teacher from Tyne and Wear. At the height of Roxy Music's popularity, the band would wear fantastically louche outfits, balanced perfectly by Price: embellished tights, marabou feathers and fur shrugs, emerald-green metallic jackets, tiger-print shirts, sequined biker jackets and skin-tight trousers, and the occasional off-the-shoulder leopard-print vest. In many ways, Roxy Music was a brand. It had a crafted, art-directed look, with music videos, live performances, iconic album covers and merchandise all perfectly calibrated. In later years, Roxy Music – and Ferry as a solo artist – evolved from glam-rock pretensions to slick suiting. Ferry's look became elegant and more than a little seductive.

Although Price's influence is undeniable, Ferry has always had an interest in fashion and art. He worked in a tailor's shop when he was 16, becoming obsessed with stylebooks and fashion illustrations, and studied under Pop artist Richard Hamilton at Newcastle University. Today Ferry sports a tailored, considered look; he makes the occasional appearance at fashion shows, is impressively design-literate and is considered something of an expert in sartorial matters.

Creating an enduring pop look has always been sink or swim, but Bryan Ferry perfectly understands the relationship between music and fashion. Ferry experimented with his style early on in his career, but by the time of this portrait (by a hotel pool in Tokyo, 1983) his dressing had evolved into a love of upscale suiting.

PRINCE

Performer, writer and producer, Prince Rogers Nelson (1958–2016) is the American music industry powerhouse, the flamboyant creative genius whose explorations in R&B, rock, pop, hip-hop, jazz and disco have produced some of the world's most recognizable (and erotic) pop music of the past three decades. His personal style and theatrical on-stage look are intertwined.

Prince's first album, *For You*, released in 1978, had moderate success, but his self-titled follow-up in 1979 went platinum and the artist became an international star, as he rapidly evolved his musical and visual style. His songs used sexually explicit lyrics and his on-stage and off-stage style grew more experimental; Prince is famous for maintaining creative control. By the mid-1980s he wore paisley or sequined suits and delicate frilly shirts, his hair teased up into a messy pompadour, accessorized with jewels, fingerless lace gloves and candy-coloured furs – a cartoonish Minnesotan New Romantic with huge 1980s shoulder pads.

Prince's 1984 album release, *Purple Rain*, included an accompanying rock musical drama directed by Albert Magnoli. It was Prince's film debut and received positive reviews, and the financial success of the project underpinned the founding of his own Paisley Park Studios. The film's marketing images – Prince's tiny form astride a motorbike, wearing a ruffled shirt and an oversized purple jacket peppered with studs – has become an iconic image in its own right. He appeared bare-chested on *Prince* and then completely naked on *Lovesexy* (1988); he wore nothing but a pair of tiny black briefs to promote his 1981 album, appropriately titled *Controversy*.

Prince attending the official premiere of *Purple Rain* on 26 July 1984 at the Mann's Chinese Theater in Hollywood, California. Dressed in full sparkly regalia – in homage to his character, the Kid, in the film – the financial success of the project was a turning point for Prince, allowing him to take even more control of his artistic output.

RIVER PHOENIX   c.1990

At the time of his death, 23-year-old actor River Phoenix (1970–93) was one of Hollywood's brightest rising stars. Seemingly destined to forge a career in parallel to Brad Pitt or Leonardo DiCaprio, Phoenix had already been nominated for an Academy Award and was being considered for a number of heavy-duty roles.

Phoenix was the ultimate teen idol with a troubled past. His family lived in poverty in Florida and joined a cult in Venezuela before returning to the United States. He and his four younger siblings were spotted busking in Los Angeles by a children's agent, who set their careers in motion. Phoenix's films punctuated late-1980s and early-1990s teen culture. *Stand by Me* (1986) was perhaps his breakout role, and he received an Academy Award nomination for Best Supporting Actor for *Running on Empty* (1988).

My Own Private Idaho (1991) was perhaps Phoenix's most seminal film, Gus Van Sant's low-budget Shakespeare-inspired indie buddy movie, also starring Phoenix's friend Keanu Reeves. The young actors' styling in this film was greatly influenced by the grunge and skate scene, and was immortalized in a landmark Bruce Weber shoot for *Interview* magazine. As Mike Waters, in the film, Phoenix wears a perfectly calibrated indie uniform: a vintage Sherpa lined corduroy jacket with gas-station work shirt and beanie, or a James Dean-style pea coat with skater T-shirt. In an iconic scene with Reeves on a motorbike, Phoenix is seen behind him, wearing a grubby, louche-looking red-and-tan cotton jacket, holding on to his friend.

This rare shoot by John Roca, in the sunshine of Central Park, New York, shows the young actor in a vintage floral Western shirt. Photographers always sought to underline Phoenix's left-field, thrift-store style, a perfect rendering of the laid-back grunge look of the early 1990s.

Phoenix as Mike Waters in a film still from *My Own Private Idaho* (Gus Van Sant, 1991), wearing battered, mismatched vintage workwear that evokes a melancholy Americana – and a strong sense of 1990s nostalgia.

IAN BROWN

As front man of The Stone Roses, Ian Brown (1963–) presided over the Manchester indie scene in the late 1980s and early 1990s. Influenced by alternative rock, electronic dance music and psychedelia, The Stone Roses – and their peers Happy Mondays, The Charlatans and Inspiral Carpets – were the stars of a northern England drug-fuelled music and fashion subculture that dominated the music press.

Brown's band formed in 1983 and released its eponymous debut album in 1989. A breakthrough success, Brown soon became an international star noted for his unique approach to style. He drew from baggy hip-hop styling and wore it with a 1960s-influenced, northern England 'scally' sensibility, dressing in Adidas tracksuits, bucket hats and Stone Island sweatshirts. It was this unique style – loose or flared jeans, hippie tie-dye T-shirts, bucket hats, references to casual sportswear and rave – that earned the Manchester sound the nickname 'baggy' music.

With sharp, angular features, high cheekbones, a mop of dark, long hair, and a reputation for moodiness and near-silence in interviews, Brown had a veneer of toughness. The Stone Roses broke up in 1996, but Brown relaunched as a solo artist, holding on to his 'Madchester' look, and even to his long hair. This steadfastness to a personal style – with a three-stripe leather Adidas tracksuit as his mainstay – is as much appreciated by the music press as by Brown's ageing fan base.

Ian Brown performing with The Stone Roses at the band's infamous Spike Island gig on 27 May 1990. Brown was at the heart of the Manchester sound, the music and style movement that was an unlikely meshing of creative influences from 1960s psychedelia to hip-hop style, drug culture and the upscale sportswear of the 'New Casuals'.

The lofty, spindle-limbed musician, voice actor, author and radio presenter Jarvis Cocker (1963) is considered one of the most important figures of Britpop. As the unlikely front man of indie pop outfit Pulp, and later as a solo artist, Cocker's sinuous, jolting dance style, floppy hair and skinny suits have become his trademark.

Vintage thrift-store suiting was the core of Cocker's early style; he wore wool, tweed, velvet or corduroy slim-cut double- or single-breasted jackets, sometimes with flares. Rich, off-beat 1960s- and 1970s-inspired purples, mustards, dark greens and sludge browns formed his go-to colour palette, and he wore ties, messily knotted, and sometimes high-heeled shoes. Cocker subverted the dominant, showy pop star style with charity-shop finds and markedly 'uncool' items, to create a unique, geeky look that was easy for Pulp fans to copy.

Cocker's style has remained constant; his brand of geography teacher chic has served him well into middle age. His solo career has been a success but, as a radio presenter and talking head, he remains a true British eccentric for whom the public feels great affection. His stage invasion during Michael Jackson's Brit Awards performance in 1996 – a sudden protest at Jackson's portrayal of himself as a Christ-like figure – prompted many to suggest that Cocker should be knighted.

As the Sheffield-born front man of Britpop mega-band Pulp, Jarvis Cocker is known for his charity-shop chic. Sludge-coloured suits accentuated his thin frame, while patterned shirts and accessories made him seem like the world's coolest geography teacher.

As front man of The Smiths (from 1982 to 1987) and then as a cultish solo performer, Steven Patrick Morrissey (1959–) made poetry of staid British suburban culture, dealing in kitchen-sink realism and the drama of domesticity. His wry, sardonic take on the mainstream, coupled with an upbeat, indie pop sound, spoke to an isolated, disillusioned youth.

Morrissey has steadfastly held on to a look that has changed only slightly through the decades, and which is typified by a tall sprig of dark hair. From the early days, Morrissey's messy, teased-up pompadour was his only touch of flamboyance. The Smiths' look was decidedly unflashy – downbeat knits, crumpled shirts, jeans and Morrissey's famous dark-rimmed specs. On stage, his only theatrical concessions were Smiths T-shirts and a straggly bunch of flowers that he wafted about as he sang, or had poking out of his back pocket.

Morrissey launched his solo career in 1988 with the album *Viva Hate*, considered a landmark moment in British music and seen as laying down the foundations for Britpop. In the early to mid-1990s Morrissey fleshed out his waif-like indie persona into something more overtly masculine: the cover art for *Your Arsenal* (1992) showed him bare-chested with a gym-toned body. This subtle shift – a growing up of sorts – has allowed Morrissey's fans to age with him; his uniqueness as a creative, particularly as a lyricist, has created a furiously loyal fan base, many of whom have been there from the beginning.

December 1992 and Salford's pop poet Steven Patrick Morrissey wears a typically downbeat outfit. He had already begun a successful solo career – the album *Your Arsenal*, released earlier that year, scored a Grammy nomination – and Morrissey's style was soon to develop into a more overtly masculine look.

KURT COBAIN 1993

American musician and tragic hero Kurt Cobain (1967–94) was the lead singer, guitarist and main songwriter of Nirvana, the cultish outfit at the heart of the early-1990s Seattle music scene. At the height of Cobain's career, Nirvana was one of the most recognizable bands in the world, and his relationship with singer Courtney Love made for a punk-edged power couple. Critically and commercially successful, Cobain struggled with addiction and depression and had an uneasy relationship with the trappings of fame. He committed suicide in 1994.

Cobain's personal style typified a dark-edged American slacker look: he wore mismatched, oversized outfits with loose-cut denim, baggy cardigans, vintage shirts and striped T-shirts, topped with perfectly messy long hair. As biographers squabble over Nirvana's grunge status, the fashion world has always found the genre a powerful reference. In 1992 Marc Jacobs showed a grunge-inspired collection for Perry Ellis, considered one of his career-defining moments, and contemporary designers and brands return to grunge for inspiration time and time again.

In charting Cobain's look, there are particular images that resound: in 1992 he wore a T-shirt proclaiming 'Corporate Magazines Still Suck' on the cover of *Rolling Stone*, and a 'Hi, How Are You?' T-shirt by musician Daniel Johnston to the 1992 MTV Video Music Awards (the shirt print is still being produced due to high demand). In September 1993 Cobain was photographed by David Sims for the cover of *The Face* wearing a baggy floral dress – styled with eyeliner – while photographer Mark Seliger's famous solitary Polaroid, a black-and-white headshot taken during a shoot for *Rolling Stone*, shows a young man, unguarded and fragile.

Music photographer Stephen Sweet's 1993 portrait of Kurt Cobain in front of conceptual artist Barbara Kruger's *Men Don't Protect You Anymore* installation. Cobain's 'thrift-store slacker' look inspired a generation of teenage grunge kids.

PETER BEARD

American artist, photographer and diarist Peter Beard (1938–) is celebrated for his pictures of African wildlife, handmade photo-collage works (sometimes smeared with his own blood). He is also known for his salacious playboy past that features Studio 54, supermodels, friendships with artists Andy Warhol and Francis Bacon, the highs and lows of drugs, and paying off bar tabs with his own artworks.

Over the decades, Beard's look has remained somewhat constant – snaps of him taken in smoky 1970s clubs right up to modern times show a suited, preppy party-goer, or an outdoorsy man in khakis and shirts. There are also rugged sepia shots of a young Beard in a rough sweater or soft furs, always relaxed and effortlessly handsome.

Childhood international travel ignited the artist's love of Africa, while Beard's moneyed upbringing allowed him a place in New York creative society, and his personal style often bridges these two worlds. His marriage to model and actress Cheryl Tiegs (from 1982–6) made him a darling of the fashion world, and he took portraits of Mick Jagger and David Bowie, slowly becoming a style icon himself. In alternate photos, he is the modern-day adventurer, grinning and athletic (he has navigated crocodile-infested waters and been gored and, on different occasions, thrown by a charging rhinoceros and elephant), a louche Studio 54 stalwart in a tangle of supermodel limbs, and the quiet bohemian artist working on his journals.

Beard's works have been exhibited and published since the 1970s, and today he divides his time between his Kenyan ranch and estate in Montauk, Long Island. His art career has, at times, been eclipsed by his own personal style.

This 1995 portrait, by Chris Felver, of the American artist and New York socialite Peter Beard shows him wonderfully laid-back, scruffy and off-duty in Montauk, Long Island, a world away from the upscale supermodel-studded parties he often frequented.

JOHN WATERS

Cult film-maker and *bon vivant* John Waters (1946–) is affectionately known as the 'Pope of Trash'. Spindle thin with a wisp of cropped hair and trademark pencil-thin moustache, Waters is the director of low-budget gross-out flicks including *Pink Flamingos* (1972), which starred the wonderfully grotesque drag superstar Divine. The unique visual character of his films, books and artworks is synonymous with his personal style – deliciously dark, playful and off-kilter.

Waters spent his childhood in Lutherville, Maryland, the kind of humdrum American suburb that has featured in many of his works, fuelling his obsession with trash culture and the bored 1950s teen subculture known as greaser. His early films deal with bad girls from the wrong side of the tracks, all bravado and bosoms, their *mise en scène* characterized by a lurid, candy-coloured palette. His own wardrobe reflects his rebellious spirit, peppered with loud prints and bright suits worn with sneakers and a wry smile.

In recent times, budgets and bureaucracy have slowed down Waters's cinematic output – he hasn't made a film since 2004's *A Dirty Shame*. Instead, he has starred in documentaries, toured comedic one-man shows, put on art shows and hitchhiked across America for his 2014 book *Carsick*. With his dedicated fan base and effortless wit, the self-appointed 'King of Bad Taste' remains a truly colourful character.

Slick and suited film-maker John Waters presides over his own creative genre, a hyperreal mashup of 1950s kitsch, suburban melodrama and gross-out culture that has had a huge influence on fashion and style.

HAMID KARZAI

At the beginning of Tom Ford's term of office as creative director of Yves Saint Laurent as well as Gucci, the designer marked out Hamid Karzai (1957–) as the 'chicest man on the planet today', while fashion writer Glenn O'Brien lauded the president of Afghanistan as having 'a real sense of style'. Politicians are not generally known for their dress sense, but Karzai has harnessed the visual power of fashion to great ends.

Born into a politically active family, Karzai became a dominant figure in Afghan politics following the removal of the Taliban regime in late 2001, was interim president from 2002, and then president for two full terms (2004–14). He is always impeccably groomed with a clipped grey beard, and wears a crisp grey or white cotton *perahan tunban*, a traditional and rather modest banded-collar tunic with matching trousers. On top sits a perfectly cut suit jacket or patterned *chapan* robe in jewel-bright tones, and then – Karzai's trademark accessory – a *karakul* hat, a charcoal-grey topper made from Karakul lamb's wool. As president of Afghanistan, Karzai needed to project an image of authentic tribal lineage, modesty and power, with a little ceremonial pomp to maintain a strong presence in international diplomacy.

There is a strong element of tradition to Karzai's outfits (his *chapan* robes draw influence from the Uzbek communities of northern Afghanistan), and his wearing of the *karakul* has a pleasingly defiant old-fashioned edge – it was last popular as a men's accessory in the 1960s and 1970s.

Hamid Karzai, then the Afghan Interim Authority Chairman, on a trip to Washington, DC, in 2002. He wears a traditional *chapan* robe and *karakul* hat – a look that balanced the sartorial expectations of both international contemporary politics and his tribal ancestry.

TOM WOLFE

In 1962 the American writer and journalist Tom Wolfe (1931–) elected to wear a white silk twill summer suit in winter. Teamed with a homburg hat and two-tone shoes, it served to get him noticed as he made his move from Richmond, Virginia, to New York City. The white suit became Wolfe's trademark throughout most of his career, and to it the writer attributes his ability to get a scoop and appear interesting in interviews. Wolfe's personal style, gentlemanly yet jarring, marked him as an outsider and provocateur, and his most famous literary works, *The Electric Kool-Aid Acid Test* (1968) and *The Bonfire of the Vanities* (1987), are testament to this.

In many ways, Wolfe is the surveyor of American culture, exploring male power and the decaying of the American Dream, but also the nature of journalism itself. His bending of literary conventions produced celebrated experimental writings and the innovation of New Journalism, a free-form style of journalism that started with the story 'The Kandy-Kolored Tangerine-Flake Streamline Baby', published in *Esquire* in 1963, focusing on what he saw as the unbridled one-upmanship of the decade. Wolfe's viewpoint is always from the outside, the odd man out with a natural curiosity to see things as they really are. How better to mark your difference than spending a lifetime in a white silk suit?

Author Tom Wolfe, pictured here in his Upper East Side apartment in New York City, October 2004. Wolfe's neat trick of getting noticed and being memorable, while underlining his outsider approach as a writer, was to always wear a crisp white suit.

NIGO

Japanese fashion designer Nigo (born Tomoaki Nagao; 1970–) is the one-time drummer and Bunka Fashion College graduate who worked as a fashion stylist for *Popeye* magazine before setting up his own brand in 1993, in Harajuku, Tokyo. He is the poster boy for streetwear couture, those cultish, limited-edition skate-influenced brands that deal in hoodies, T-shirts and caps. Through his brand, A Bathing Ape (named in homage to his favourite film, Franklin J Schaffner's *Planet of the Apes*, 1968) and also known as Bape, Nigo's reimagining of simple, essential jersey items with cartoonish prints was adroit; for two years he created a small weekly run of T-shirts, selling some and seeding others among influential friends. But it was Nigo's clever business model of limited supply that created feverish demand – and made the young designer a multimillionaire and fashion celebrity, scoring the cover of the Asian edition of *Time* magazine in 2004.

Although he is notoriously shy and modest about his achievements, at the height of his success Nigo lived large; alongside his own designs he wore the chunky diamond jewellery of a hip-hop star with flat-peak caps and beanies, and has diamond-encrusted teeth. After leaving the brand in 2013 and taking on new design roles, Nigo's style has somewhat tempered, shifting from SpongeBob SquarePants loopiness to a slim, trim functionality via dark denim, shirts and worker jackets.

Japanese designer and streetwear supremo Nigo outside the Louis Vuitton store on the Champs-Elysées, Paris, in 2005. The previous year he had made the cover of Asian *Time* magazine and to this day retains a cult following among streetwear devotees.

COLIN FIRTH

In the late 1980s Colin Firth (1960–) was a member of the Brit Pack, a group of young, slightly posh actors chosen by *The Face* magazine as the rising stars of contemporary UK cinema. By 1995 Firth had scored the lead role in a BBC television version of *Pride and Prejudice*, his Mr Darcy placing him firmly at the heart of UK costume drama and kick-starting a hugely successful cinema career.

On screen he remains terribly British, cast in dramatic and comedic roles that riff on the idea of the stiff upper lip, where a man's true nature is perpetually drowning in a stodge of manners, etiquette and tradition. From the *Bridget Jones* trilogy (2001, 2004, 2016) to *The King's Speech* (2010), for which he won an Academy Award, and *Tinker Tailor Soldier Spy* (2011), Firth has been dressed in an impeccable wardrobe of classic suiting, his look evolving naturally towards luxury and heritage brands.

Off screen Firth cuts a fine figure as a contemporary British 'gent'. Like the characters he plays, the actor tends to wear the very best in suiting, occasionally softening it with knitwear or denim, a modern and wonderfully unfussy yet luxury look. Firth's defining moment in style was his decision to accept the lead role in fashion designer Tom Ford's 2009 adaptation of Christopher Isherwood's novel, *A Single Man*. Costume designer Arianne Phillips dressed Firth in elegant slim-cut, early-1960s suiting, which was set against dark, luxury interiors created by the production team behind the successful American television series *Mad Men*. Firth's personal style jumped up a notch, his face now framed by vintage-look eyewear.

Although the British actor had gained everlasting screen-idol status as Mr Darcy in the 1995 BBC adaptation of *Pride and Prejudice*, it was Tom Ford's *A Single Man* (2009), in which he played a grieving California college professor, that secured Colin Firth's style credentials.

PETER MARINO

In a profession that deals in incomprehensible budgets and projects that can take years – decades, even – to reach their tangible conclusion, you might imagine a formal and slightly staid personal style to dominate. Peter Marino (1949–), the legendary leather-clad architect, is the exception. Since founding his New York-based practice in 1978, Marino has created hundreds of retail spaces for luxury brands, from Chanel to Louis Vuitton – and he has done it all in fetish-inspired, thick-cut black leather and rubber.

Marino's unique approach to style might be explained by his unconventional past. As a self-confessed Factory kid, Marino was a sometime member of Andy Warhol's inner circle, and architect of the late artist's Upper East Side townhouse. Inheriting Warhol's pop sensibility, Marino took on retail projects and private rooms and residences in his early years, commissions that were anathema to other architects, and worked with renowned New York department store Barneys in the 1980s. With retail architecture now a respected and excitingly experimental genre of design, Marino can be considered, in part, to be its forefather.

This taboo-breaking, defiant approach is best seen in Marino's personal style – he is the ultimate power dresser, a Tom of Finland leather daddy, complete with black cop hat, dark glasses, tight T-shirts, leather armbands and tattoos. Now in his mid-sixties, Marino projects the confidence of a man whose success, creatively and personally, is unshakable. On the red carpet he remains a flamboyant presence, cutting through the manicured perfection of his contemporaries with a pair of glossy leather chaps or a handmade leather harness, pouting and smiling for the camera.

Black leather, zips and studs: award-winning architect Peter Marino has an unshakably consistent style. His unique sexualized look communicates power and status, and is a shortcut to ensuring that he always stands out.

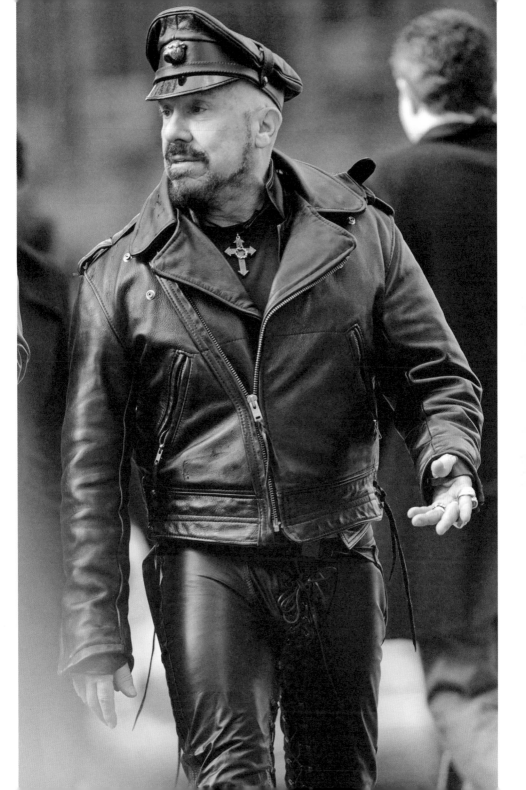

WES ANDERSON

To understand the quirky personal style of director Wes Anderson (1969–), look to his catalogue of meticulously art-directed films. From *The Royal Tenenbaums* (2001) and *The Darjeeling Limited* (2007) to *Moonrise Kingdom* (2012) and *The Grand Budapest Hotel* (2014), his fast-paced, whimsical comedies tinged with melancholy have a unique, nostalgic visual sensibility.

As a child in Texas, Anderson made silent movies using Super-8 film, worked as a part-time cinema projectionist and studied philosophy at the University of Texas at Austin, where he met his friend and collaborator, actor and writer Owen Wilson. Anderson quickly turned the camera on his own life in his early film *Rushmore* (1998), using his own school in Houston as a location. Although the biographical element is integral to Anderson's work, it is his highly original visual and editing style that marks the director out.

A rich and varied wardrobe of lounge suits, wool tweeds, linens and velvet blazers look loose and unstructured on Anderson's willowy frame. He wears shirts and ties, or simple crew-neck knits in muted colours; there is something defiantly 'uncool' about the director's style. He wears his hair long, crystal-framed eyewear and desert boots, and is every inch as quirky as the characters he creates on screen. Even his stop-action animation film of Roald Dahl's 1970 book, *Fantastic Mr. Fox* (2009), full of suited woodland creatures, has a costume design reminiscent of Anderson himself.

A promotional portrait of the director in 2014, in his trademark wool tweed suit, shirt and crew-neck knit, a purposefully quirky, timeless look.

The official poster of Anderson's stop-motion animation, *Fantastic Mr. Fox* (2009). Spot the director's personal style.

YOHJI YAMAMOTO

In the late 1970s and early 1980s three Japanese designers set the fashion world alight with their ground-breaking avant-garde designs: Issey Miyake (1938–), Comme des Garçons' Rei Kawakubo (1942–) and Yohji Yamamoto (1943–). Although Yamamoto had founded his own label Y's in Tokyo in 1972, it was his debut show in Paris nine years later – a key moment in contemporary fashion design – that marked Yamamoto as a truly unique talent at odds with the Establishment.

Yamamoto graduated from Keio University in 1966 with a law degree but did not want to work as a lawyer. Instead, he worked for his mother, a dressmaker, who then suggested he attend Bunka Fashion College. His landmark 1981 show in Paris was a work of pure avant-garde bravura: asymmetric, loose-fitting, mostly devoid of colour and downbeat. Yamamoto showed a brave indifference not only to trends but also to gender conventions – sexuality, even. The fashion press struggled to describe Yamamoto's work, calling it 'the crow look' or 'Hiroshima chic', but the young designer's enduring influence had been set in motion.

Since the beginning of his career Yamamoto's personal style has been a constant. He is always swamped in blacks and inky blues, billowing overcoats and waistcoats, a simple white shirt and refined double-breasted suiting worn with long dark hair, a wide-brimmed hat, loose-fit trousers, indie-edged tennis shoes and a cloud of cigarette smoke. In the late 1980s Yamamoto achieved a black belt in karate, his athletic bent leading him to collaborate with Adidas on Y-3, a sportswear brand almost as famous as his own.

Japanese designer Yohji Yamamoto – in his imposing trademark outfit – on the catwalk after his Autumn/Winter 2015 men's collection presentation for Y-3 at Paris Fashion Week.

KANYE WEST

Pop-culture polymath, writer, rapper and producer, art collaborator and fashion designer, Kanye West (1977–) is one of the most lauded musical artists ever. His mastery over a wide range of genres and creative media is undeniable, but it is arguably his unshakable self-belief that has garnered him a loyal fan base, rolling press attention and more than his fair share of critics.

West began to produce for artists at Roc-A-Fella Records in 2000 while working on his own rap album in his spare time. His debut album, *The College Dropout* (2004), was a critical and commercial success. His popularity grew, and further releases, exploring surprisingly different musical influences, showed West's ability to shock both critics and fans.

West's approach to fashion has evolved and he has openly shown his eagerness to learn – sometimes by making mistakes. In this way, West's personal style is mercurial and has ranged from upscale luxury brands to the utilitarianism of tonal, skate-inspired sportswear and – more recently – the designs of Raf Simons, Maison Margiela and Katharine Hamnett.

In 2009 he collaborated with Nike on the cultish Air Yeezy sneakers and put his name to a shoe line for Louis Vuitton. His two fashion collections, shown at Paris Fashion Week in 2011 and 2012, had mediocre reviews at best, but his slick Adidas Originals Collection, launched in 2015, with a presentation staged by artist Vanessa Beecroft, was warmly received.

The world's most divisive polymath leads the formation at the Kanye West x Adidas Fall/Winter collection show at New York Fashion Week, in what was part fashion show, part Vanessa Beecroft-staged performance art.

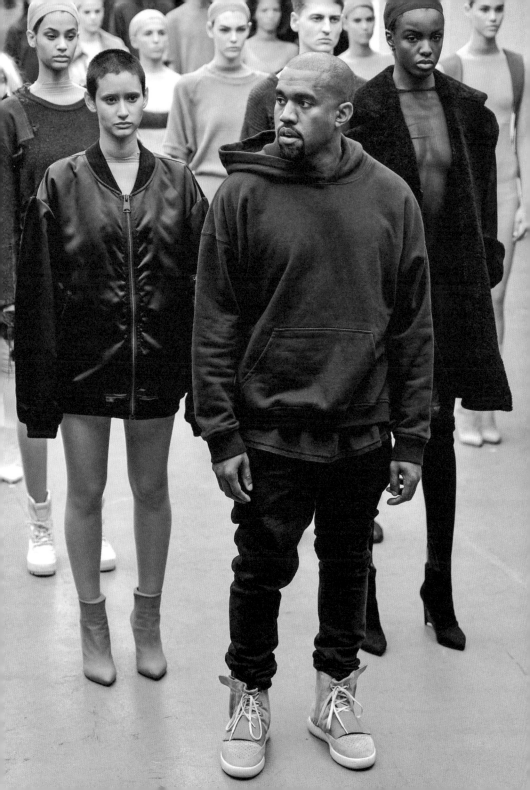

WARIS AHLUWALIA

As a jewellery designer, pop-up restaurateur, film producer, writer and actor, Waris Ahluwalia (1974–) is a true creative… and difficult to define. Ahluwalia has created the House of Waris, the brand under which he realizes most of his projects. There he presents his fine jewellery and updates on his latest creative endeavours – a short film made in collaboration with director Luca Guadagnino, for instance, or an article for *The Paris Review*.

Born in Amritsar, India, into a family of academics, Ahluwalia moved to New York as a child, wore heavy-metal T-shirts as a teenager, cowboy boots (steel-toed with a skull and crossbones on the tip) as a college student, and slowly became interested in style and creativity. He started House of Waris after appearing as Vikram Ray in his friend Wes Anderson's film *The Life Aquatic with Steve Zissou* (2004) and his personal style evolved. The film's costumier, Milena Canonero, introduced Ahluwalia to real tailoring, and slick, expertly cut suits have become a key feature of his look, putting him on Best Dressed lists.

Although Ahluwalia's black turban and beard set him apart in a creative scene woefully lacking in diversity (his Sikh faith traditionally requires a turban and forbids shaving), his footwear remains a clever quirk: he is rarely without his salmon-pink desert boots, custom-made by designer George Esquivel.

Film actor, producer and writer, jewellery-maker and event supremo Waris Ahluwalia sporting his favourite accessory, his pale-pink desert boots, at this dinner in New York, April 2015.

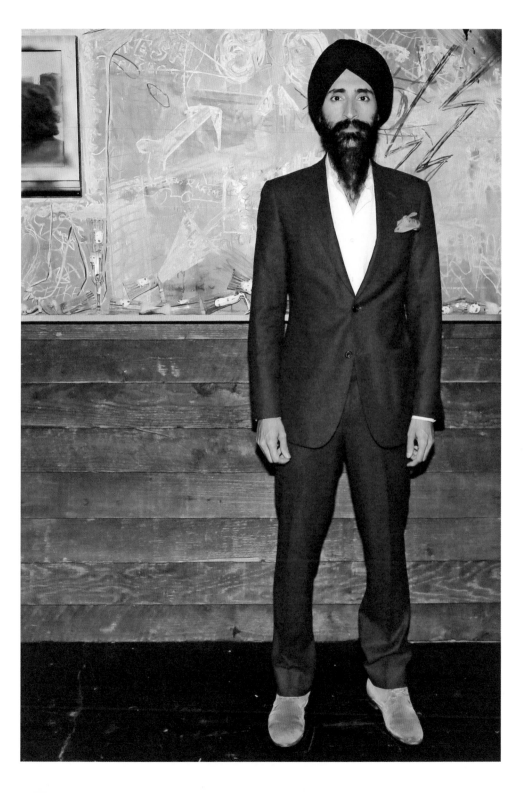

NICK WOOSTER

American fashion consultant, Instagram superstar, accessories designer and style savant, Nickelson Wooster (1960–) is a thoroughly modern icon. A fixture at style events, from New York Fashion Week to legendary Italian men's trade show Pitti Immagine Uomo, Wooster's perfectly groomed silver hair and beard, hipster tattoos and modern-classic outfits cause the same frantic scramble of street-style snappers outside fashion shows that is usually reserved for the female front-row crowd.

Wooster's background in advertising, fashion buying and merchandising – and a lifelong love of fashion – has helped prepare him for his current incarnation as street-style icon and brand collaborator. Two portraits of Wooster at Milan Fashion Week in 2010 – one by Scott Schuman, the other by Tommy Ton, both hugely popular photo-bloggers – saw Wooster thrown into the spotlight. A few years later, Wooster can now score thousands of Instagram Likes wearing almost any outfit – from a bespoke three-piece suit with cropped trousers to a crumpled pair of swim shorts and a short-sleeve shirt.

Although Wooster has always been something of a snappy dresser, he is one of the few men who have achieved fame for their personal style later in life. The Manhattan-dweller uses his amassed style knowledge to collaborate with his favourite international and sometimes obscure brands, designing capsule collections, consulting and advising; he also blogs about his travels and the items he would love to own.

As a star of Instagram and street-style blogs, influential style icon Nick Wooster is pictured in countless perfectly styled outfits, usually cutting a dash at international fashion weeks. Here, he is looking rather fresh at the Ferragamo show in Milan, in June 2015.

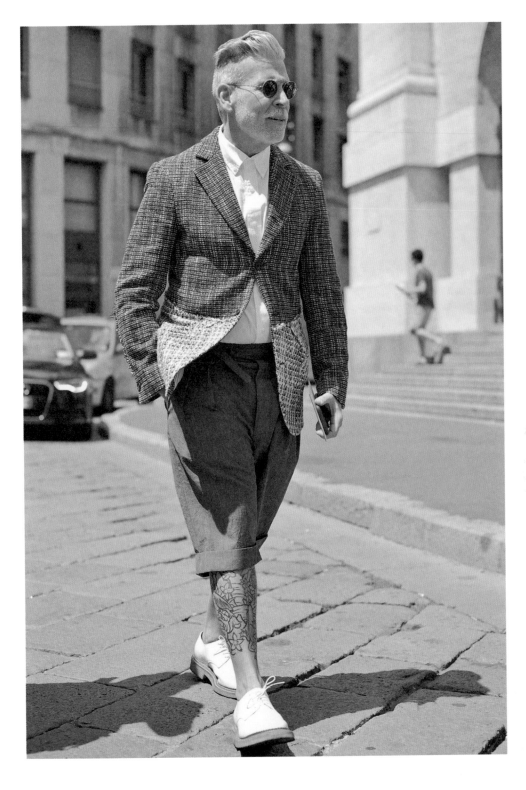

DAVID BECKHAM

Not so long ago, when David Beckham (1975–) changed his hairstyle, men the world over would change theirs with him. In the early days of Beckham's on- and off-pitch career, 1990s lad culture was at its peak and the handsome soccer star was its leading celebrity. With his masculinity underpinned by a macho day job, Beckham found himself able to experiment with style – (almost) always to a powerful, trend-making effect. Why else would the men of Britain – and further afield – invest in a hairband, or even a sarong?

Modern masculinity, and how it is communicated, has grown with Beckham, using him as a signifier. Now in his forties and retired from professional sport, he is more likely to generate celeb content by looking after his children at one of his wife Victoria's fashion shows than by raising hell as a beered-up ex-footballer. A quiet confidence is communicated via a more mature, considered way of dressing; gone are the days of choppy bleach jobs and 'his and her' matching red-carpet outfits. Beckham's current look is all about iconic, classic dressing with a worldly edge: white T-shirts and tattoos, crisp suiting with a little stubble, or luxury heritage brands with his own David Beckham H&M underwear underneath.

Of the many incarnations of Beckham's personal style, his contemporary look – smart, suited and rough around the edges – is perhaps his most confident. Here, he is pictured at the Wimbledon Championships in July 2015.

A rarity: David Beckham in a Prada suit in 1997, one of his first forays into modelling.

GRAYSON PERRY

Grayson Perry (1960–) is the British artist with real punk credentials who works with printmaking, drawing, embroidery and ceramics, using traditionally soft, craft-edged media to explore difficult or controversial concepts. His projects have included a series of ceramic urns (for which he won the Turner Prize in 2003), tapestries that deal with the British obsession with class, and *Julie's House*, a full-sized holiday home in Essex. His most captivating creation, however, is Claire, his female persona who has her own spectacular wardrobe of embellished princess frocks.

Perry has dressed as a woman, part-time, since he was a teenager, but it was his appearance as Claire at the Turner Prize award ceremony in 2003 that made the artist synonymous with cross-dressing. His own style trajectory seems to have been influenced by his Essex upbringing, his family's early rejection of his cross-dressing, sharing a house with milliner Stephen Jones and singer Boy George, and going to Blitz, the legendary London club night. He also worked with the Neo Naturists, an art performance group that fought back Thatcherism and fashionistas alike with decidedly unfashionable hippie nudity and messy, upbeat happenings.

In Claire's early days, the baby-doll dresses and impossibly frilly petticoats marked her out as an obvious construct, a flimsy character we could easily see through to the artist inside. Yet Perry's Claire has enjoyed many incarnations since her notable debut in 2003, from slick businesswoman to leather-bound dominatrix: her once-blousy look has become refined and her appearance at upscale art events has become a much-anticipated necessity.

The artist reclining at Chatsworth House, Derbyshire, in 2015. Perry has a long and artful history of dressing up as his alter ego, Claire, now a firm fixture on the gallery circuit.

INDEX

PICTURE CREDITS

CREDITS

An Hachette UK Company
www.hachette.co.uk

First published in
Great Britain in 2016 by
Conran Octopus, a division
of Octopus Publishing
Group Ltd, in conjunction
with the Design Museum

Octopus Publishing
Group Ltd
Carmelite House
50 Victoria Embankment
London EC4Y 0DZ
www.octopusbooks.co.uk
www.octopusbooksusa.com

Distributed in the US by
Hachette Book Group
1290 Avenue of the
Americas, 4th and 5th Floors,
New York, NY 10020

Distributed in Canada by
Canadian Manda Group
664 Annette St., Toronto,
Ontario, Canada M6S 2C8

A CIP catalogue record
for this book is available
from the British Library.

Dan Jones asserts his moral
right to be identified as the
author of this work.

Commissioning Editor:
Joe Cottington
Consultant Editor:
Deyan Sudjic
Editor:
Pollyanna Poulter
Copy Editor:
Robert Anderson
Creative Director:
Jonathan Christie
Design:
Untitled
Picture Researcher:
Nick Wheldon
Production Controller:
Allison Gonsalves

Printed and bound in China
ISBN 9-781-84091-728-4

10 9 8 7 6 5 4 3 2 1

The Design Museum is one of the world's
leading museums of contemporary design.
Design Museum Members enjoy free
unlimited entry to the museum's outstanding
exhibitions as well as access to events,
tours and discounts. Becoming a Member
is an inspiring way to support the museum's
work. Visit designmuseum.org/become-a-
member and get involved today.